D0502424

My Noiseless Entourage

My Noiseless Entourage

Poems

Charles Simic

HARCOURT, INC.

Orlando ★ Austin ★ New York ★ San Diego ★ Toronto ★ London

Copyright © 2005 by Charles Simic

All rights reserved. No part of this publication may be reproduced or
transmitted in any form or by any means, electronic or mechanical,
including photocopy, recording, or any information storage and
retrieval system, without permission in writing from the publisher.

Requests for permission to make copies of any part of the work
should be mailed to the following address: Permissions Department,
Harcourt, Inc., 6277 Sea Harbor Drive, Orlando, Florida 32887-6777.

www.HarcourtBooks.com

Library of Congress Cataloging-in-Publication Data
Simic, Charles, 1938–
My noiseless entourage: poems / Charles Simic.—1st ed.
p. cm.
I. Title.
PS3569.I4725M9 2005
811'.54—dc22 2004025586
ISBN 0-15-101214-8

Text set in Dante MT
Designed by Liz Demeter

Printed in the United States of America

First edition   ·
A C E G I K J H F D B

To Helen

CONTENTS

I

II

III

IV

My Noiseless Entourage

I

DESCRIPTION OF A LOST THING

It never had a name,
Nor do I remember how I found it.
I carried it in my pocket
Like a lost button
Except it wasn't a button.

Horror movies,
All-night cafeterias,
Dark barrooms
And poolhalls,
On rain-slicked streets.

It led a quiet, unremarkable existence
Like a shadow in a dream,
An angel on a pin,
And then it vanished.
The years passed with their row

Of nameless stations,
Till somebody told me *this is it!*
And fool that I was,
I got off on an empty platform
With no town in sight.

SHADING EXERCISE

This street could use a bit of shade
And the same goes for that small boy
Playing alone in the sun,
A shadow to dart after him like a black kitten.

His parents sit in a room with shades drawn.
The stairs to the cellar
Are hardly used any more
Except for an occasional prowler.

Like a troop of traveling actors dressed to play *Hamlet,*
The evening shadows come.
They spend their days hidden in the trees
Outside the old courthouse.

Now comes the hard part:
What to do with the stones in the graveyard?
The sun doesn't care for ambiguities,
But I do. I open my door and let them in.

SELF-PORTRAIT IN BED

For imaginary visitors, I had a chair
Made of cane I found in the trash.
There was a hole where its seat was
And its legs were wobbly
But it still gave a dignified appearance.

I myself never sat in it, though
With the help of a pillow one could do that
Carefully, with knees drawn together
The way she did once,
Leaning back to laugh at her discomfort.

The lamp on the night table
Did what it could to bestow
An air of mystery to the room.
There was a mirror, too, that made
Everything waver as in a fishbowl

If I happened to look that way,
Red-nosed, about to sneeze,
With a thick wool cap pulled over my ears,
Reading some Russian in bed,
Worrying about my soul, I'm sure.

TO DREAMS

I'm still living at all the old addresses,
Wearing dark glasses even indoors,
On the hush-hush sharing my bed
With phantoms, visiting the kitchen

After midnight to check the faucet.
I'm late for school, and when I get there
No one seems to recognize me.
I sit disowned, sequestered and withdrawn.

These small shops open only at night
Where I make my unobtrusive purchases,
These back-door movie houses in seedy neighborhoods
Still showing grainy films of my life.

The hero always full of extravagant hope
Losing it all in the end?—whatever it was—
Then walking out into the cold, disbelieving light
Waiting close-lipped at the exit.

THE GAMBLERS UPSTAIRS

That faint rattle of dice rolling
Late at night
No one else hears—
They are wagering over me, placing bets,

The high rollers and their sidekicks
On their knees.
Little Joe from Baltimore,
Ada from Decatur.

The noise of bones,
The hush after each roll
Keeping me awake—
God's throw or devil's?

My love holding her hands over my eyes
As we inch toward the stairs
Stripped down to our underwear
And liable to slip and break our necks.

CALAMITY CRIER

Of this much you can be sure:
Shadow lengthening among shadows
Of other hurried pedestrians,
The more innocent you believe you are,
The harder it'll be for you.

In this store window full of musical instruments,
I could not make out their faces
Nor could they make out mine.
Golden trumpets accustomed to blowing dust,
I thought, and turned my back with a shudder.

What a grand parade of phantoms—
Or were they mourners?
Carrying signs made illegible by the darkness
And the sun going down
Setting the pawnshops on fire.

THE ALARM

The hundreds of windows filling with faces
Because of something that happened on the street,
Something no one is able to explain,
Because there was no fire engine, no scream, no gunshot.
And yet here they all are assembled.
Some with hands over their children's eyes,
Others leaning out and shouting
To people walking the streets far below
With the same composure and serene appearance
Of those going for a Sunday stroll
In some other century, less violent than ours.

MY NOISELESS ENTOURAGE

We were never formally introduced.
I had no idea of their number.
It was like a discreet entourage
Of homegrown angels and demons
All of whom I had met before
And had since largely forgotten.

In time of danger, they made themselves scarce.
Where did they all vanish to?
I asked some felon one night
While he held a knife to my throat,
But he was spooked too,
Letting me go without a word.

It was disconcerting, downright frightening
To be reminded of one's solitude,
Like opening a children's book—
With nothing better to do—reading about stars,
How they can afford to spend centuries
Traveling our way on a glint of light.

FABULOUS SPECIES AND LANDSCAPES

That chill breath you felt
On your neck,
That long arm
Out of undertaker's basement,

It snatched your watch.
You saw its feathers fly,
Wings darken,
Or were they rat's whiskers?

You even saw your ears disappear
In its pocket.
Churchwarden's ears
Pinched raw with cold.

★

Dustball alchemists
Under the bed,
Cobweb wigmakers,
Mirrors never looked at.

A tongue by itself
In a birdcage
Covered with a blue work shirt
For the night, asking:

How many minutes
In a glass of water
By the bedside?
How many slow sips?

★

Blood too which flows
Like a stream
In the woods
While you sleep.

You're a leaf floating
In its rushes,
You are the white foam
And the cataract,

A river that doesn't know its name
And the sea at night
Like a trinket peddler setting up its stall,
And the moon a pork butcher.

★

The belly hobbles
In wooden clogs
Using a knife and fork
As crutches

While you sit
Like a rain puddle in hell
Knitting the socks
Of your life.

The world dreams of you
Buttoned up to the chin
Turning on a spit
With an apple in your mouth.

USED CLOTHING STORE

A large stock of past lives
To rummage through
For the one that fits you
Cleaned and newly pressed,
Yet frayed at the collar.

A dummy dressed in black
Is at the door to serve you.
His eyes won't let you go.
His mustache looks drawn
With a tip of a dead cigar.

Towers of pants are tilting,
As you turn to flee,
Dead men's hats are rolling
On the floor, hurrying
To escort you out the door.

THE CENTURIES

Many a poor wretch left no trace
Of ever having lived here.
This punch bowl made of silver
Belonged to a house with turrets.
It's still standing—though the rose garden
And the birch trees are long gone.

The stone walls deep in the woods
Tell another story, how everything
Foretold in dreams came to pass:
The young woman huddled on her bed
Naked and trembling with cold
Still wearing the veil she wore in church.

The small girls admiring watch faces
In the window of a jewelry store
Cannot yet tell time—and neither can I.
Come spring, our roads are muddy.
The news of the outside world arrives
More quickly but still finds us mystified.

VOYAGE TO CYTHERA

I'll go to the island of Cythera
On foot, of course,
I'll set out some May evening,
Light as a feather,
There where the goddess is fabled to have risen
Naked from the sea—

I'll jump over a park fence
Right where the lilacs are blooming
And the trees are feverish with new leaves.
The swing I saw in a painting once
Is surely here somewhere?

And so is the one in a long white dress,
With eyes blindfolded
Who gropes her way down a winding path
Among her masked companions
Wearing black capes and carrying daggers.

This is all a dream, fellows,
I'll say after they empty my pockets.
And so are you, my love,
Carrying a Chinese lantern
And running off with my wallet
In the descending darkness.

❧ II ❧

USED BOOK STORE

Lovers hold hands in never-opened novels.
The page with a recipe for cucumber soup is missing.
A dead man writes of his happy childhood on a farm,
Of riding in a balloon over Lake Erie.

A sudden draft shuts his book in my hand,
While a philosopher asks how is it possible
To maintain the theologically orthodox doctrine
Of eternal punishment of the damned?

Let's see. There may be sand among the pages
Of a travel guide to Egypt or even a dead flea
That once bit the ass of the mysterious Abigail
Who scribbled her name teasingly with an eye pencil.

HITCHHIKERS

after a Walker Evans photograph from the thirties

Hard times brought them out early
On this dreary stretch of road
Carrying a suitcase and a bedroll
With a frying pan tied to it,
The kind you use over a campfire
When a moss-covered log is your pillow.

He's hopeful and she's ashamed
To be asking a stranger to take them
Away from here in a cloud of flying
Gravel and dust, past leafless trees
With their snarled and pointy little twigs.
A man and a woman catching a ride
To where water tastes like cherry wine.

She'll work as a maid or a waitress,
He'll pump gas or rob banks.
They'll buy a car as big as a hearse
To make their fast getaway,
Not forgetting to stop for you, mister,
If you are down on your luck yourself.

GRAVEYARD ON A HILL

Let those who so desire continue to dream
Of heavenly mansions
With their vast chambers and balconies
Awash in the light of a golden afternoon.

I'll take this January wind, so mean
It permits no other thought
Than the one that acknowledges its presence
Among these weedy tombstones
And these trees out of a vampire flick
Bending to the breaking point

And then straightening up—intact,
With the wind busy elsewhere,
Nudging dead leaves to take a few quick hops
Right up to the branch they fell from.

THE WORLD RUNS ON FUTILITY

Sea waves destined to repeat themselves,
Forever stammering excuses
To the gulls lining up your shores.
Or you, gusting wind, troubling these pines
With your wild oratory.

Even you, coming darkness,
And you tumbleweeds rolling over,
Through a ghost town
With the bug that lives one day
On a torn window screen
And a sky full of white clouds.

One torn photograph after another
Whose pieces do not fit—
And why should they, grim whispers,
With all your seasonings of folly?
Every time I went to the sea and sky
To seek advice, this is what I got.

BATTLING GRAYS

Another grim-lipped day coming our way
Like a gray soldier
From the Civil War monument
Footloose on a narrow country road.
A few homes lately foreclosed,
Their windows the color of rain puddles
About to freeze, their yards choked
With weeds and rusty cars.

Small hills like mounds of ashes
Of your dead cigar, general,
Standing bewhiskered and surveying
What the light is in no hurry
To fall upon, including, of course,
Your wound, red and bubbling
Like an accordion, as you raise your saber
To threaten the clouds in the sky.

SUNLIGHT

As if you had a message for me...
Tell me about the grains of dust
On my night table?
Is any one of them worth your trouble?

Your burglaries leave no thumbprint.
Mine, too, are silent.
I do my best imagining at night,
And you do yours with the help of shadows.

Like conspirators hatching a plot,
They withdrew one by one
Into corners of the room.
Leaving me the sole witness
Of your burning oratory.

If you did say something, I'm none the wiser.
The breakfast finished,
The coffee dregs were unenlightening.
Like a lion cage at feeding time—
The floor at my feet turned red.

THE BIRDIE

Two-room country shack
On a moody lake.
A black cat at my feet
To philosophize with

Stretched out on the bed
Like a gambler
Who's lost his trousers
And his shoes,

Listening to a birdie raise its voice
In praise of good weather,
Little wiggling worms,
And other suchlike matters.

MINDS ROAMING

My neighbor was telling me
About her blind cat
Who goes out at night—
Goes where? I asked.

Just then my dead mother called me in
To wash my hands
Because supper was on the table:
The little mouse the cat caught.

COCKROACH SALON

The clips of the scissors
And the voices
Difficult to discern at first
Even as I press my ear against the wall.

The barber and his customer
Talking of greasy spoons,
Late night back alleys,
Rats leaping out of trash cans

Then, nothing further...
Had they wandered off
Deeper into the wall,
Or possibly inside my head?

Where else? Where else?
Someone replied cheerfully,
Her identity and whereabouts
A complete mystery, a scandal.

MIDNIGHT FEAST

for Michael Krüger

Snowflake and laughter salad.
Cuckoo-clock soup.
Andouillettes of angel and beast.
Bowlegged nightingale in aspic.

Peep-show soufflé.
Fricassee of Cupid with green peas.
Roasted bust of Socrates with African postage stamps.
Venus in her own gravy.

Wines of graveyard lovers—
Or so I read in a take-out menu
Someone slid under my door
While I sat staring at the wall.

ONE CHAIR

That can't help creak at night
As if a spider
Let itself down
By a thread
To hang over it
With the chair quaking
At the outcome.

INSOMNIA'S CRICKET

I'll set you up in a tiny cage over my pillow.
You'll keep me company,
Warn me from time to time
As the silence deepens.

My father spent nights in the bathroom
Thinking about the meaning of his life.
We'd forget all about him,
Find him asleep there in the morning.

O cunning walls, ceilings
And mirrors in the dark,
I heard his pocket watch tick on his grave—
Or was it a cricket?

In the same tall grass
Where eternity was being made
By a few solitary fireflies
In the tails of someone's black coat.

TALK RADIO

"I was lucky to have a Bible with me.
When the space aliens abducted me...."

America, I shouted at the radio,
Even at 2 A.M. you are a loony bin!

No, I take it back!
You are a stone angel in the cemetery

Listening to the geese in the sky
Your eyes blinded by snow.

❈ III ❈

MY TURN TO CONFESS

A dog trying to write a poem on why he barks,
That's me, dear reader!
They were about to kick me out of the library
But I warned them,
My master is invisible and all-powerful.
Still, they kept dragging me out by the tail.

In the park the birds spoke freely of their own vexations.
On a bench, I saw an old woman
Cutting her white curly hair with imaginary scissors
While staring into a small pocket mirror.

I didn't say anything then,
But that night I lay slumped on the floor,
Chewing on a pencil,
Sighing from time to time,
Growling, too, at something out there
I could not bring myself to name.

THE HERMETICAL AND ALCHEMICAL WRITINGS OF PARACELSUS

Any man or woman, this book tells me,
Can bring an egg to maturity under the arm,
Materializing thus in a wonderful fashion
What may seem to you wildly beyond belief.

If the parents have large ears and long noses,
That helps. Large ears are a sign of good memory
And brainpower, while a long nose denotes
A farsighted person, secretive but fair.

The newly hatched chickens walk
The yard with their eyes cast down
Looking for precious stones in the dirt
With which they hope to repay their parents.

As for a rooster procreated in such manner,
It inclines to idleness and frivolous pursuits,
Gaining whatever livelihood it can get
At state fairs and seaside penny arcades.

ON THE FARM

The cows are to be slaughtered
And the sheep, too, of course.
The same for the hogs sighing in their pens—
And as for the chickens,

Two have been killed for dinner tonight,
While the rest peck side by side
As the shadows lengthen in the yard
And bales of hay turn gold in the fields.

One cow has stopped grazing
And has looked up puzzled
Seeing a little white cloud
Trot off like a calf into the sunset.

On the porch someone has pressed
A rocking chair into service
But we can't tell who it is—a stranger,
Or that boy who never has anything to say?

I SEE LOTS OF STICKS ON THE GROUND

Do people still whittle around here?
Do they carry clasp knives for that purpose?
Do they sit on porches and tree stumps
With shavings piling up at their feet?

Are dogs keeping a close eye on them?
Do they lay their heads on their paws
And sigh as the stick gets shorter?
What thoughts are they thinking as they whittle?

Little thoughts about many little things,
Or big thoughts about one big thing?
Come dark, is there enough of a stick left
To sit back and chew on a toothpick?

EVERYBODY HAD LOST TRACK OF TIME

The wide-open door of a church.
The hearse with one flat tire.
The grandmother on the sidewalk
Leaning on a cane and cupping her ear.

The lodger no one has ever seen,
Drawing her bath upstairs.
The little boy who climbed on the roof
To keep the clouds company.

An old man carrying a chair
And a rope into the backyard
As if he meant to hang himself
And then sat down and lost track of time.

BRETHREN

A woodpecker hammers
On the gutter of a nursing home
Where the war cripple sits
In a wheelchair by the gate.

The windows are wide open,
But no one ever speaks here,
Neither about the crazy bird,
Nor about that other war.

ASK YOUR ASTROLOGER

My stars have been guilty of benign neglect.
They neither procure riches for me
Nor burn my house down.
They've left me dangling halfway
Between good and bad luck.

A predicament I cannot afford to treat casually.
I'm all on edge. I look over my shoulder.
There goes some deadbeat
Stepping on shadows of pedestrians
As if they were scurrying mice.

I have to go into a church to avoid him.
To our Lord who has withdrawn
Into a corner with his wounds
I say, that world out there
Is a riddle even you can't solve.

Afterward, the coast clear, I rush to buy
A newspaper and read my horoscope.
A diet of small disappointments and minor
Contentments is to be my lot for the week,
Unless, of course, the astrologer blew it.

KAZOO WEDDING

The groom is red-cheeked as he blows into a kazoo
And so is the bride as she blows one too.
The guests are blowing hundreds of kazoos
And the Minister as he prepares to bless their union.
The weeping bridesmaid covers her ears.
One sounds like a bad muffler on a hearse,
Another like a wedding dress ripped open at midnight.
Look, even our Lord on the cross is tooting a kazoo!
What are they playing? the hard of hearing are asking.
It's a wedding march, Grandpa, the ushers shout.

SNOWY MORNING BLUES

The translator is a close reader.
He wears thick glasses
As he peers out the window
At the snowy fields and bushes
That are like a sheet of paper
Covered with quick scribble
In a language he knows well enough,
Without knowing any words in it,

Only what the eyes discern,
And the heart intuits of its idiom.
So quiet now, not even a faint
Rustle of a page being turned
In a white and wordless dictionary
For the translator to avail himself
Before whatever words are there
Grow obscure in the coming darkness.

TO FATE

You were always more real to me than God.
Setting up the props for a tragedy,
Hammering the nails in
With only a few close friends invited to watch.

Just to be neighborly, you made a pretty girl lame,
Ran over a child with a motorcycle.
I can think of a million similar examples.
Ditto: How the two of us keep meeting.

A fortune-telling gumball machine in Chinatown
May have the answer,
An old creaky door opening in a horror film,
A pack of cards I left on a beach.

I can feel you snuggle close to me at night,
With your hot breath, your cold hands—
And me already like an old piano
Dangling out of a window at the end of a rope.

SLURRED WORDS

Taking cover in the closet
With my dark suspicions.
Two of her nightgowns brush my cheeks
As I stand trembling.

At the funeral, I thought I had much to say,
When in truth I had nothing.
I was just one more crow
Trailing after the pallbearers.

This house is haunted,
Though I've never seen a ghost.
I don't count myself, of course,
Or their bare feet in bed,

Incubus, spreading his black wings
Over her in the slow afternoon hours
As she lay writhing
Like a snake at the end of a stick.

MEETING THE CAPTAIN

In one of these old seaside towns,
On soot-stained December afternoons
When it's wise to hurry home
Past the closed-up summer homes,
While he hugs the shadows in pursuit.

I caught a glimpse of him once
Towering in his stovepipe hat
At the top of the stairs to my room
With its view of the sky at sunset
Washing its bloody rags in the sea.

Looking for stowaways under my bed,
Runaway orphans, pot lickers
In wooden clogs, rat and mice catchers
And finding, instead, Melville's book
And a gull moping on the windowsill.

SWEETEST

Little candy in death's candy shop,
I gave your sugar a lick
When no one was looking,
Took you for a ride on my tongue
To all the secret places,

Trying to appear above suspicion
As I went about inspecting the confectionary,
Greeting the owner with a nod
With you safely tucked away
And melting to nothing in my mouth.

LEAVES AT NIGHT

Talking to themselves, digressing, rambling on—
Or is it a tête-à-tête we are overhearing?
A flutter of self-revelations, a gust of recriminations
With the moon slipping in and out of the clouds.

A half-mad oak tree affronted by nature's conduct,
The vagaries of New England weather.
The foolish adoration of every skimpy ray of sunlight,
Or some other disturbing truth?

A mock-heroic farce being played in whispers.
The tree as the hanging judge, the tree as the accused.
Windy night squabble followed by a long hush
As they wait anxiously for our applause.

⁕ IV ⁕

STARLINGS IN A TREE AT DUSK

Spooked me. They had heard a rumor
We had not yet,
And were collectively
On the verge of panic.

The few of us passing the park
Quickened our steps,
With a wary, sidelong glance
At each other.

Bent under some obscure burden,
We were fleeing,
Crossing the avenue and dispersing
As if we, too, had wings.

THE HEADLINE

The way you sat at the kitchen table
Made you look like you were staring at your feet
Or thinking of the next move
On an invisible chessboard.

Truth to tell, you were doing neither.
It was seven o'clock in the morning.
You were waiting for a ray of sunlight
To warm your cold feet,

Or your wife to amble in drowsily
In her frayed blue bathrobe,
And reach down with hair over her eyes
For the paper that had slid out of your hands
With its headline and large picture,

And remain like that, bent over, reading
Intently, with her robe opening bit by bit,
The dangling breast and dark pubic hair
Still moist with sleep coming into full view,
While she read on in that ghastly whisper.

THE TRAGIC SENSE OF LIFE

Because few here recall the old wars,
The burning of Atlanta and Dresden,
The great-uncle who lies in Arlington,
Or that Vietnam vet on crutches
Who tried to bum a dime or a cigarette.

The lake is still in the early morning light.
The road winds; I slow down to let
A small, furry animal cross in a hurry.
The few remaining wisps of fog
Are like smoke rising out of cannons.

In one little town flags fly over dark houses.
Outside a church made of gray stone,
The statue of the Virgin blesses the day.
Her son is inside afraid to light a candle,
Saying, *Forgive one another, clothe the naked.*

Niobe and her children may live here.
As for me, I don't know where I am—
And here I'm already leaving in a hurry
Down a stretch with little to see,
Dark woods everywhere closing in on me.

THE ROLE OF INSOMNIA IN HISTORY

Tyrants never sleep a wink:
An aggrieved and grim
Unblinking eye
Stares back at the night.

The mind is a palace
Walled with mirrors.
The mind is a country church
Overrun with mice.

When dawn breaks,
The saints kneel,
The tyrants feed their hounds
Chunks of bloody meat.

IN THE PLANETARIUM

Never-yet-equaled, wide-screen blockbuster
That grew more and more muddled
After a spectacular opening shot.
The pace, even for the most patient
Killingly slow despite the promise
Of a show-stopping, eye-popping ending:
The sudden shriveling of the whole
To its teensy starting point, erasing all—
Including this bag of popcorn we are sharing.

Yes, an intriguing but finally irritating
Puzzle with no answer forthcoming tonight
From the large cast of stars and galaxies
In what may be called a prodigious
Expenditure of time, money and talent.
"Let's get the fuck out of here," I said
Just as her upraised eyes grew moist
And she confided to me, much too loudly,
"I have never seen anything so beautiful."

IN THE MORNING HALF-AWAKE

A memory of a cloudless summer sky,
The elegant boredom of trees
On a slow, windless day.
The quiet of little-traveled country roads
Crisscrossed by shadows.

The house with curtains drawn,
A pair of red slippers on the front steps,
But no one in the barn
Or among the roses, which like being greeted
And admired this early.

Love, that damn fool, who points a flashlight
With a dying battery into the past
Ought to find more than a goat
Tied to a stake ready to butt anyone
Should they dare to step his way.

THE ABSENTEE LANDLORD

Surely, he could make it easier
When it comes to inquiries
As to his whereabouts.
Rein in our foolish speculations,
Silence our voices raised in anger,

And not leave us alone
With that curious feeling
We sometimes have
Of there being a higher purpose
To our residing here
Where nothing works
And everything needs fixing.

The least he could do is put up a sign:
AWAY ON BUSINESS
So we could see it,
In the graveyard where he collects the rent
Or in the night sky
Where we address our complaints to him.

HE HEARD WITH HIS DEAD EAR

Your prayer. The one you offered
On behalf of someone ailing.
Darkness was his world,
So you shut your eyes tight to come into it.

There was no one there.
He may be wearing another disguise,
You were told.
No one can keep track.

The morning light was full of cobwebs,
As if it had brushed against a ghost.
A cow they forgot to milk
Had lowed all night long.

Now it was peaceful again.
Her bed had its sheets stripped off.
One of her red slippers missing—
In fact, nowhere to be found.

DECEMBER 21

These wars that end
Only to start up again
Somewhere else
Like barber's clippers,
Or like these winters
With their bleak days
One can trace back to Cain.

All I've ever done—
It seems—is go poking
In the ruins with a stick
Until I was covered
With soot and ashes
I couldn't wash off,
Even if I wanted to.

MY WIFE LIFTS A FINGER TO HER LIPS

Night is coming.
A lone hitchhiker
Holds up a homemade sign.

Masked figures
Around a gambling table?
No, those are scarecrows in a field.

At the neighbors',
Where they adore a black cat,
There's no light yet.

Dear Lord, can you see
The fleas run for cover?
No, he can't see the fleas.

OUR OLD NEIGHBOR

Who hasn't been seen in his yard
Or sitting on his front porch
For what seems like forever,
Whose house stays dark at night,
The garage closed, the great
Hearse of a car parked in the back.

Whom, nevertheless, we suspect
Of spying on us at all hours
From behind drawn curtains,
His absence and our alleged presence
Casting shadows on the street
Of almost identical homes

Where an odd rush wind in the leaves
Now and then makes us imagine
We are hearing muffled voices
Where in truth there is no one,
Only an upstairs window partly open
Over his surprisingly well-kept lawn.

PIGEONS AT DAWN

Extraordinary efforts are being made
To hide things from us, my friend.
Some stay up into the wee hours
To search their souls.
Others undress each other in darkened rooms.

The creaky old elevator
Took us down to the icy cellar first
To show us a mop and a bucket
Before it deigned to ascend again
With a sigh of exasperation.

Under the vast, early-dawn sky
The city lay silent before us.
Everything on hold:
Rooftops and water towers,
Clouds and wisps of white smoke.

We must be patient, we told ourselves,
See if the pigeons will coo now
For the one who comes to her window
To feed them angel cake,
All but invisible, but for her slender arm.

Some of these poems have previously appeared in the following magazines, to whose editors grateful acknowledgment is made: *The New Yorker*, *The London Review of Books*, *Poetry*, *The Gettysburg Review*, *TLS*, *The Iowa Review*, *Jubilat*, *The New England Review*, *Literary Imagination*, and *Tri-Quarterly*.

BOSTON PUBLIC LIBRARY

3 9999 05365 313 3